HAL•LEONARD
pro vocal®
BETTER THAN KARAOKE!

ADELE

2ND EDITION

SING 8 POP HITS WITH SOUND-ALIKE AUDIO TRACKS

T0066171

PLAYBACK+
Speed • Pitch • Balance • Loop

To access audio visit:
www.halleonard.com/mylibrary

Enter Code
8370-1592-1785-6083

Chasing Pavements

Words and Music by Adele Adkins and Francis Eg White

leads no - where? _ Or would it be a waste, e - ven if I knew my place? Should I

leave it there? _ Should I give up or should I just keep chas-in' pave-ments,

e - ven if it leads no - where? _____ I

Verse

build my-self up ___ and fly a-round in cir-cles, wait-in' as my heart _ drops, _ and my

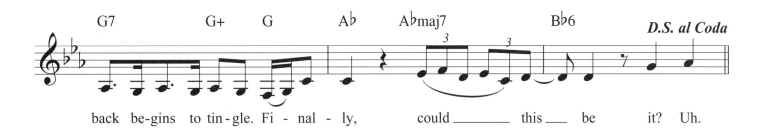

back be-gins to tin-gle. Fi - nal - ly, could _____ this ___ be it? Uh.

Coda

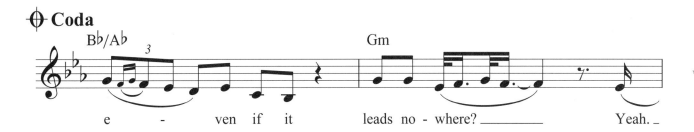

e - ven if it leads no - where? _____ Yeah. _

Bridge

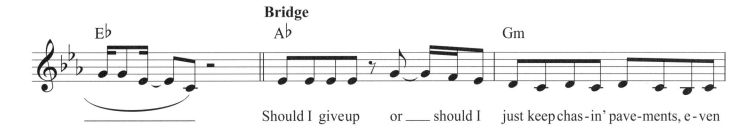

_____ Should I give up or ___ should I just keep chas-in' pave-ments, e - ven

Make You Feel My Love

Words and Music by Bob Dylan

Intro
Moderately slow

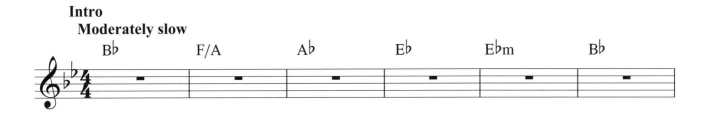

When the rain ___ is blow-in'

in your face ___ and the whole ___ world ___ is on ___ your case, ___

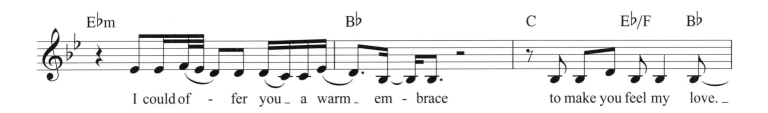

I could of - fer you ___ a warm ___ em - brace to make you feel my love. ___

Verse

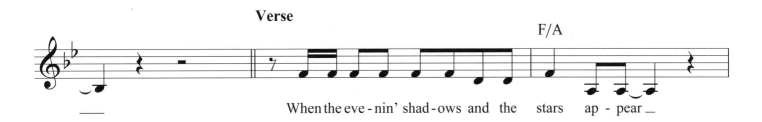

___ When the eve-nin' shad-ows and the stars ap - pear ___

and there is no ___ one there to dry ___ your ___ tears, ___ I could hold ___ you for ___ a

mil - lion years _____ to make you feel my _ love. _

Bridge

I know you have-n't made your mind up yet, _ but I would nev-er do _ you wrong. _

_ I've known it from the mo - ment _ that we _ met, _

Verse

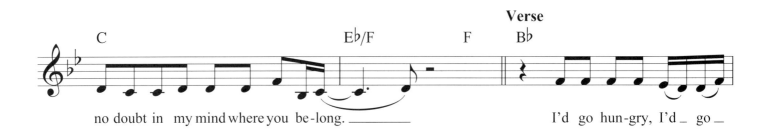

no doubt in my mind where you be-long. _____ I'd go hun-gry, I'd _ go _

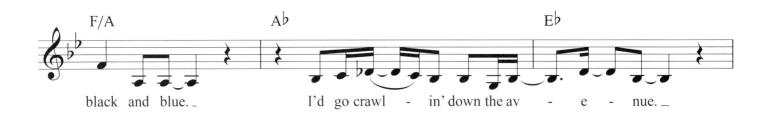

black and blue. _ I'd go crawl - in' down the av - e - nue. _

No, there's noth-ing that _ I _ would-n't do _____ to make you feel my love. _

Interlude

Bridge

The storms are rag-ing on the roll-in' sea___ and on the high-way of re-gret.___

___ The winds of change are blow-in'___ wild and free._____

Verse

You ain't seen noth-in' like me yet. I could make you hap-py, make___ your___

dreams come true.___ Noth-ing that I,___ I would-n't___ do.___

Go to the ends of___ the___ earth for you___ to make you feel my_____ love,___

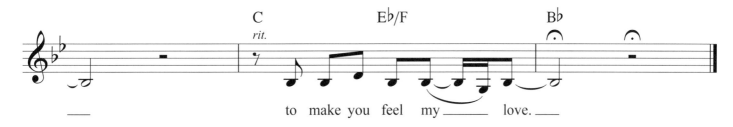

___ to make you feel my_____ love.___

Hello

Words and Music by Adele Adkins and Greg Kurstin

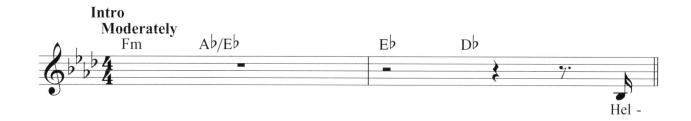

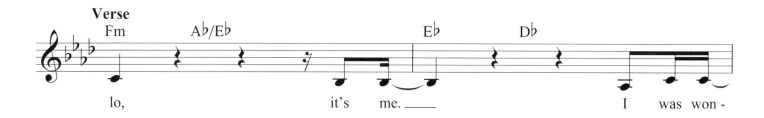

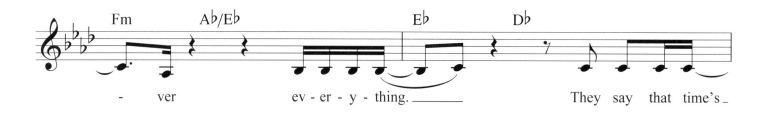

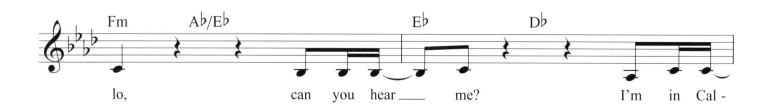

Verse

12

I'm sor - ry for break - ing your heart. But it don't mat -

ter: it clear - ly does-n't tear you a - part ___ an - y - more. ___

Interlude

___ Ooh, _____ an - y - more. ___
(Have, have have, have, love, love, love, love.)

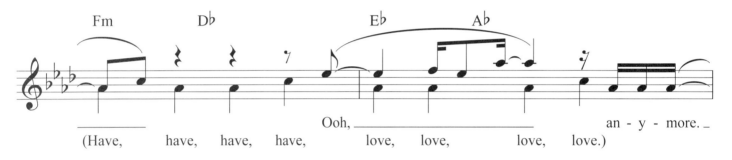

___ Ooh, _____ an - y - more. ___
(Have, have, have, have, love, love, love, love.)

___ Ooh, _____ an - y - more.
(Have, have, have, have, love, love, love, love.)

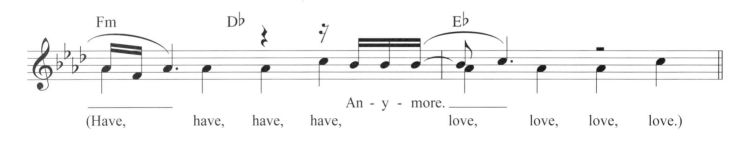

___ An - y - more. _____
(Have, have, have, have, love, love, love, love.)

Chorus

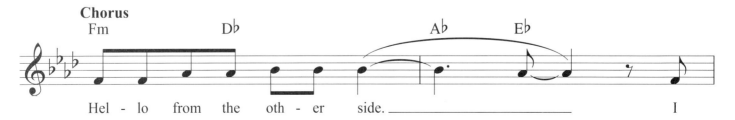

Hel - lo from the oth - er side. _____ I

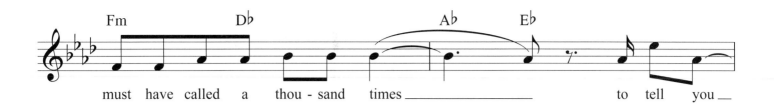

must have called a thou-sand times _____ to tell you __

____ I'm sor - ry for ev-'ry-thing that I've done, _ but when I call _

____ you nev - er seem to be home. _____

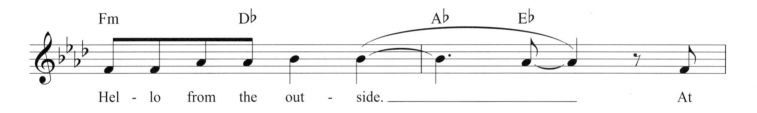

Hel - lo from the out - side. _____ At

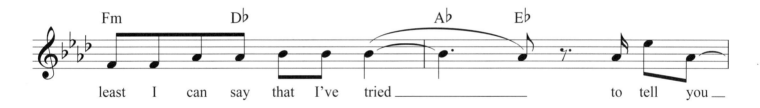

least I can say that I've tried _____ to tell you __

____ I'm sor - ry for break-ing your heart. _ But it don't mat -

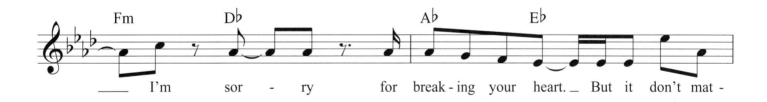

ter: it clear - ly does-n't tear you a - part __ an - y - more. __

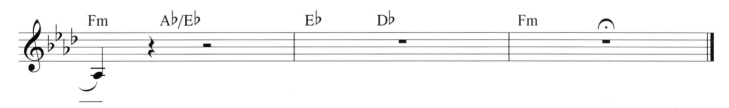

Rolling in the Deep

Words and Music by Adele Adkins and Paul Epworth

Bb5 I've heard ____ one of you, and I'm gon-na make your head burn.

C5 Think of ___ me _____ in the depths of your de-spair, **G5**

Bb5 mak - ing __ a home down there, as **G5** mine sure won't be shared. **Bb5** *D.S. al Coda*

Coda

Chorus

Bb _____ Could-'ve had it all, **Ab** _____ **Bb** roll-in' in the

Cm deep. _____ **Bb** You had my heart in - side **Ab** your hand, _

Bb _____ but you played _ it with a beat - ing.

Verse

N.C. Throw your _ soul __ through ev-er-y o-pen door, count your _ bless - ings to

C5 find what you look for. Turn my _ sor - row in - to treas-ured gold, you'll

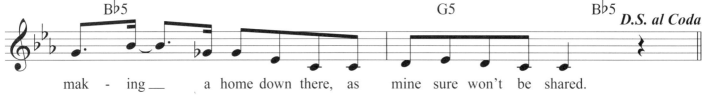

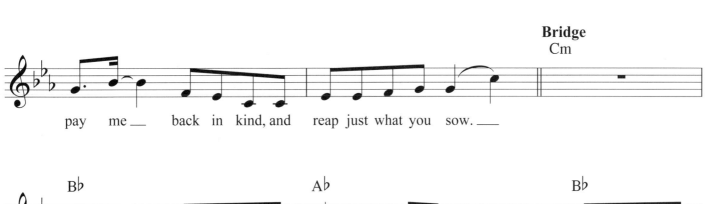

pay me ___ back in kind, and ___ reap just what you sow. ___

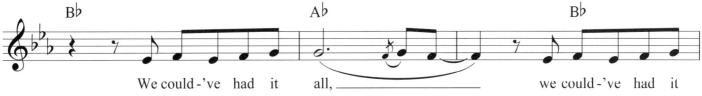

We could-'ve had it all, _____ we could-'ve had it

all, _____ it all, _____ it all, _____ it all. _

_____ We could-'ve had it all, _____ roll-in' in the

deep. _____ You had my heart in - side your hand, _

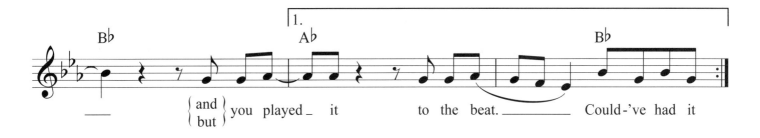

___ { and / but } you played ___ it to the beat. _____ Could-'ve had it

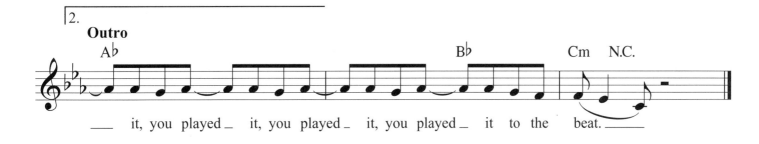

___ it, you played ___ it, you played ___ it, you played ___ it to the beat. _____

Set Fire to the Rain

Words and Music by Adele Adkins and Fraser Smith

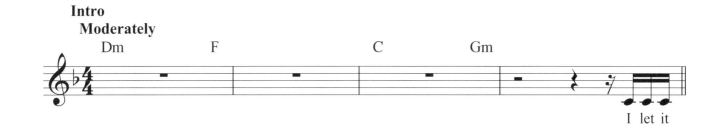

Outro

Skyfall

from the Motion Picture SKYFALL

Words and Music by Adele Adkins and Paul Epworth

Someone Like You

Words and Music by Adele Adkins and Dan Wilson

I could-n't fight it. I'd hoped you'd see my face and that you'd be re-mind-ed that for

me it is-n't o - ver.

D.S. al Coda

⊕ Coda

some-times it hurts in - stead."

Bridge

Noth - ing com - pares, no wor - ries or cares. Re - grets and mis - takes, they're

mem - o - ries made. Who would have known how bit - ter -

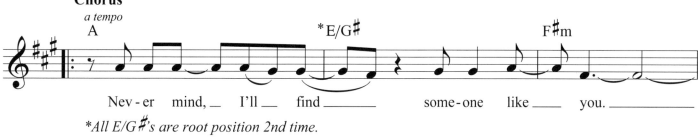

sweet this would taste?

Chorus

a tempo

Nev - er mind, I'll find some-one like you.

All E/G#'s are root position 2nd time.

I wish noth-ing but the best for

you. / you, too. "Don't for - get me," I begged.

I'll re - mem - ber you said. "Some - times it

lasts in love, but some - times it hurts in - stead." ___

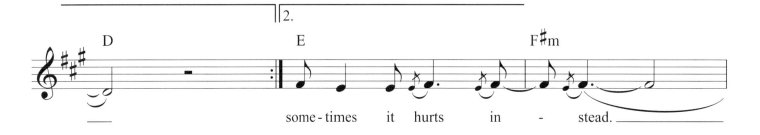

some - times it hurts in - stead. ___

Outro

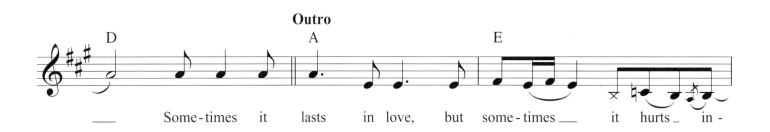

Some - times it lasts in love, but some - times it hurts in -

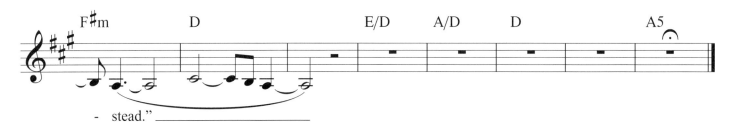

- stead." ___

When We Were Young

Words and Music by Adele Adkins and Tobias Jesso Jr.

'Cause I've been by my-self all night long, hop-ing you're

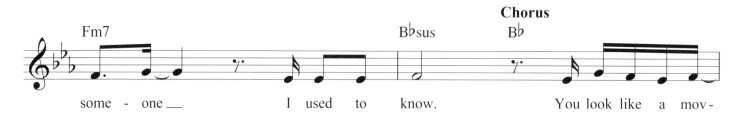

Chorus

some - one ___ I used to know. You look like a mov-

- ie, you sound like a song; my God, this re - minds ___

___ me of when we were young. Let me pho -

- to - graph ___ you in ___ this light, ___ in case ___ it is the last ___ time that we might ___

___ be ex - act - ly like ___ we were ___ be fore we re - al-ized we were sad ___

___ of get-ting old, ___ it made us rest - less. It was just like a mov-

- ie, it was just like a song.

BETTER THAN KARAOKE!

Pro Vocal® Series
SONGBOOK & SOUND-ALIKE AUDIO
SING GREAT SONGS WITH A PROFESSIONAL BAND

Whether you're a karaoke singer or an auditioning professional, the Pro Vocal® series is for you! Unlike most karaoke packs, each book in the Pro Vocal Series contains the lyrics, melody, and chord symbols for at least eight hit songs. The audio contains demos for listening, and separate backing tracks so you can sing along. Perfect for home rehearsal, parties, auditions, corporate events, and gigs without a backup band.

WOMEN'S EDITIONS
00740247	**1. Broadway Songs**	$14.95
00740249	**2. Jazz Standards**	$15.99
00740246	**3. Contemporary Hits**	$14.95
00740277	**4. '80s Gold**	$12.95
00740299	**5. Christmas Standards**	$15.95
00740281	**6. Disco Fever**	$12.95
00740279	**7. R&B Super Hits**	$12.95
00740309	**8. Wedding Gems**	$12.95
00740409	**9. Broadway Standards**	$14.95
00740348	**10. Andrew Lloyd Webber**	$14.95
00740344	**11. Disney's Best**	$15.99
00740378	**12. Ella Fitzgerald**	$14.95
00740350	**14. Musicals of Boublil & Schönberg**	$14.95
00740377	**15. Kelly Clarkson**	$14.95
00740342	**16. Disney Favorites**	$15.99
00740353	**17. Jazz Ballads**	$14.99
00740376	**18. Jazz Vocal Standards**	$17.99
00740354	**21. Jazz Favorites**	$14.99
00740374	**22. Patsy Cline**	$14.95
00740369	**23. Grease**	$14.95
00740367	**25. Mamma Mia**	$15.99
00740365	**26. Movie Songs**	$14.95
00740363	**29. Torch Songs**	$14.95
00740379	**30. Hairspray**	$15.99
00740380	**31. Top Hits**	$14.95
00740384	**32. Hits of the '70s**	$14.95
00740388	**33. Billie Holiday**	$14.95
00740389	**34. The Sound of Music**	$16.99
00740390	**35. Contemporary Christian**	$14.95
00740392	**36. Wicked**	$17.99
00740396	**39. Christmas Hits**	$15.95
00740410	**40. Broadway Classics**	$14.95
00740415	**41. Broadway Favorites**	$14.99
00740416	**42. Great Standards You Can Sing**	$14.99
00740417	**43. Singable Standards**	$14.99
00740418	**44. Favorite Standards**	$14.99
00740419	**45. Sing Broadway**	$14.99
00740420	**46. More Standards**	$14.99
00740421	**47. Timeless Hits**	$14.99
00740422	**48. Easygoing R&B**	$14.99
00740424	**49. Taylor Swift**	$16.99
00740426	**51. Great Standards Collection**	$19.99
00740430	**52. Worship Favorites**	$14.99
00740434	**53. Lullabyes**	$14.99
00740444	**55. Amy Winehouse**	$15.99
00740445	**56. Adele**	$16.99
00740446	**57. The Grammy Awards Best Female Pop Vocal Performance 1990-1999**	$14.99
00740447	**58. The Grammy Awards Best Female Pop Vocal Performance 2000-2009**	$14.99
00109374	**60. Katy Perry**	$14.99
00116334	**61. Taylor Swift Hits**	$14.99
00123120	**62. Top Downloads**	$14.99

MEN'S EDITIONS
00740250	**2. Jazz Standards**	$14.95
00740298	**5. Christmas Standards**	$15.95
00740280	**6. R&B Super Hits**	$12.95
00740411	**9. Broadway Greats**	$14.99
00740333	**10. Elvis Presley – Volume 1**	$14.95
00740349	**11. Andrew Lloyd Webber**	$14.99
00740347	**13. Frank Sinatra Classics**	$14.95
00740334	**14. Lennon & McCartney**	$14.99
00740453	**15. Queen**	$14.99
00740335	**16. Elvis Presley – Volume 2**	$14.99
00740351	**18. Musicals of Boublil & Schönberg**	$14.95
00740337	**19. Lennon & McCartney – Volume 2**	$14.99
00740346	**20. Frank Sinatra Standards**	$14.95
00740338	**21. Lennon & McCartney – Volume 3**	$14.99
00740358	**22. Great Standards**	$14.99
00740336	**23. Elvis Presley**	$14.99
00740341	**24. Duke Ellington**	$14.99
00740339	**25. Lennon & McCartney – Volume 4**	$14.99
00740359	**26. Pop Standards**	$14.99
00740362	**27. Michael Bublé**	$15.99
00740454	**28. Maroon 5**	$14.99
00740364	**29. Torch Songs**	$14.95
00740366	**30. Movie Songs**	$14.95
00740368	**31. Hip Hop Hits**	$14.95
00740370	**32. Grease**	$14.95
00740371	**33. Josh Groban**	$14.95
00740373	**34. Billy Joel**	$14.99
00740382	**36. Hits of the '60s**	$14.95
00740385	**38. Motown**	$14.95
00740386	**39. Hank Williams**	$14.95
00740387	**40. Neil Diamond**	$14.95
00740391	**41. Contemporary Christian**	$14.95
00740397	**42. Christmas Hits**	$15.95
00740399	**43. Ray**	$14.95
00740400	**44. The Rat Pack Hits**	$14.99
00740401	**45. Songs in the Style of Nat "King" Cole**	$14.99
00740402	**46. At the Lounge**	$14.95
00740403	**47. The Big Band Singer**	$14.95
00740404	**48. Jazz Cabaret Songs**	$14.99
00740405	**49. Cabaret Songs**	$14.99
00740412	**51. Broadway's Best**	$14.99
00740427	**52. Great Standards Collection**	$19.99
00740431	**53. Worship Favorites**	$14.99
00740435	**54. Barry Manilow**	$14.99
00740436	**55. Lionel Richie**	$14.99
00740439	**56. Michael Bublé – Crazy Love**	$15.99
00740441	**57. Johnny Cash**	$14.99
00148089	**58. Bruno Mars**	$15.99
00740448	**59. The Grammy Awards Best Male Pop Vocal Performance 1990-1999**	$14.99
00740449	**60. The Grammy Awards Best Male Pop Vocal Performance 2000-2009**	$14.99
00740452	**61. Michael Bublé – Call Me Irresponsible**	$14.99

00101777	**62. Michael Bublé – Christmas**	$19.99
00137717	**63. Jersey Boys**	$14.99
00109288	**64. Justin Bieber**	$14.99
00123119	**65. Top Downloads**	$14.99

EXERCISES
00123770	**Vocal Exercises**	$14.99
00740395	**Vocal Warm-Ups**	$14.99

MIXED EDITIONS
These editions feature songs for both male and female voices.
00740311	**1. Wedding Duets**	$12.95
00740398	**2. Enchanted**	$14.95
00740407	**3. Rent**	$14.95
00740408	**4. Broadway Favorites**	$14.99
00740413	**5. South Pacific**	$15.99
00740429	**7. Christmas Carols**	$14.99
00740437	**8. Glee**	$16.99
00740443	**10. Even More Songs from Glee**	$15.99
00116960	**11. Les Misérables**	$19.99
00126476	**12. Frozen**	$16.99

KIDS EDITIONS
00740451	**1. Songs Children Can Sing!**	$14.99

Visit Hal Leonard online at
www.halleonard.com

7777 W. BLUEMOUND RD. P.O. BOX 13819 MILWAUKEE, WI 53213

Disney characters and artwork © Disney Enterprises, Inc.

Prices, contents, & availability subject to change without notice.

0316

ORIGINAL KEYS FOR SINGERS

Titles in the Original Keys for Singers series are designed for vocalists looking for authentic transcriptions from their favorite artists. The books transcribe famous vocal performances exactly as recorded and provide piano accompaniment parts so that you can perform or pratice exactly as Ella or Patsy or Josh!

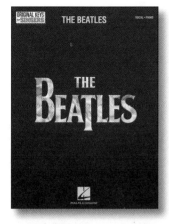

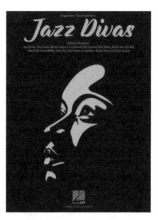

ACROSS THE UNIVERSE
00307010..$19.95

ADELE
00155395...$19.99

LOUIS ARMSTRONG
00307029...$19.99

THE BEATLES
00307400...$19.99

BROADWAY HITS (FEMALE SINGERS)
00119085...$19.99

BROADWAY HITS (MALE SINGERS)
00119084...$19.99

MARIAH CAREY
00306835...$19.95

PATSY CLINE
00740072...$19.99

ELLA FITZGERALD
00740252...$17.99

JOSH GROBAN
00306969...$19.99

GREAT FEMALE SINGERS
00307132...$19.99

GREAT MALE SINGERS
00307133...$19.99

BILLIE HOLIDAY
TRANSCRIBED FROM HISTORIC RECORDINGS
00740140...$17.99

ETTA JAMES: GREATEST HITS
00130427...$19.99

JAZZ DIVAS
00114959...$19.99

LADIES OF CHRISTMAS
00312192...$19.99

NANCY LAMOTT
00306995...$19.99

LEONA LEWIS – SPIRIT
00307007...$17.95

CHRIS MANN
00118921...$16.99

MEN OF CHRISTMAS
00312241...$19.99

THE BETTE MIDLER SONGBOOK
00307067...$19.99

THE BEST OF LIZA MINNELLI
00306928...$19.99

ONCE
00102569...$16.99

ELVIS PRESLEY
00138200...$19.99

SHOWSTOPPERS FOR FEMALE SINGERS
00119640...$19.99

BEST OF NINA SIMONE
00121576...$19.99

FRANK SINATRA – MORE OF HIS BEST
00307081...$19.99

TAYLOR SWIFT
00142702...$16.99

STEVE TYRELL – BACK TO BACHARACH
00307024...$16.99

THE BEST OF STEVE TYRELL
00307027...$16.99

SARAH VAUGHAN
00306558...$17.95

VOCAL POP
00312656...$19.99

ANDY WILLIAMS – CHRISTMAS COLLECTION
00307158...$17.99

ANDY WILLIAMS
00307160...$17.99

7777 W. BLUEMOUND RD. P.O. BOX 13819 MILWAUKEE, WI 53213

www.halleonard.com

Prices, contents, and availability subject to change without notice.

0313